NATO ARMOURED COMBAT VEHICLES

Front cover illustration: The current Infantry Fighting Vehicle of the British Army is Warrior, which equips the mechanized infantry battalions of BAOR. (Simon Dunstan)

Back cover, top: The AMX-10RC is the principal reconnaissance vehicle of the French First Army and of the *Force d'Action Rapide*. It was deployed by the French Army during Operation 'Manta' in Chad from August 1983 to November 1984.

Back cover, bottom: With its hydraulically operated crane deployed, a Challenger Armoured Repair and Recovery Vehicle (CRAAV) winches a Challenger MBT to safety during development trials. (Simon Dunstan)

NATO ARMOURED COMBAT VEHICLES

SIMON DUNSTAN

ARMS AND ARMOUR

1. The standard, wheeled Armoured Personnel Carrier (APC) of the British Army is the Saxon. Manufactured by GKN Defence, the all-welded steel hull provides protection against small arms fire, including 7.62mm armour-piercing rounds, and against artillery shell fragments. The vehicle has a crew of two, driver and commander, and up to ten infantrymen are carried.

Dedication: To TEX BA

Arms and Armour Press
A Cassell Imprint
Villiers House, 41–47 Strand, London WC2N 5JE.

Distributed in the USA by Sterling Publishing Co. Inc., 387 Park Avenue South, New York, NY 10016-8810.

Distributed in Australia by Capricorn Link (Australia) Pty. Ltd, P.O. Box 665, Lane Cove, New South Wales 2066.

British Library Cataloguing in Publication Data
Dunstan, Simon, *1949–*
NATO armoured combat vehicles
I. Title
623.7475
ISBN1-85409-027-5

Line illustrations by Tim Neate.

Designed and edited by DAG Publications Ltd. Designed by David Gibbons; edited by Michael Boxall; layout by Anthony A. Evans; typeset by Ronset Typesetters, Darwen, Lancashire; camerawork by M&E Reproductions, North Fambridge, Essex; printed and bound in Great Britain by The Bath Press, Avon.

3

INTRODUCTION

The recent events in eastern Europe have brought into sharp focus the role of the North Atlantic Treaty Organization (NATO) both within the Western Alliance and in the late 20th century. The situation is compounded by the proposals for the reduction of Conventional Forces in Europe (CFE) that are currently on the negotiating table between East and West.

This book addresses the extraordinarily diverse variety of armoured combat vehicles that operate on the modern battlefield; from self-propelled artillery pieces that commonly function approximately twenty kilometres behind the front line to the Armoured Infantry Fighting Vehicles which accompany the Main Battle Tanks into the thick of battle. In support of these strike forces is a host of vehicles that perform a myriad of tasks such as command and control; medical evacuation; air defence; logistic resupply; combat engineering; battlefield surveillance; reconnaissance; amphibious assault; anti-armour; repair and recovery; *et al*.

Throughout its existence, however, NATO has been compromised as a fighting force by the fact that many of its sixteen allies have produced in direct competition with each other families of armoured vehicles that fulfil similar roles on the battlefield. This has not only led to a duplication of effort and therefore squandering of resources, but also the potentially more costly problem of one system not being able to operate effectively with one of an ally; typically in the use of a common fuel or ammunition at the most basic level.

With the Warsaw Pact in disarray and the CFE negotiations proposing a limit of 30,000 armoured combat vehicles of the types illustrated in this volume, NATO has an unprecedented opportunity for a complete reassessment of its purpose and restructuring of its forces both in terms of numbers and weapons systems. NATO presently spends $250 billion per year on its conventional forces yet there are at least eleven firms in seven NATO countries producing anti-tank missiles and eighteen firms in seven countries developing and manufacturing anti-aircraft systems. Significant economies could be realized if NATO became a truly international force under a unified command system that also directed an integrated research and development procedure without the current wasteful duplication of effort in weapons procurement while apportioning production to the benefit of each member nation so that all could enjoy the 'Peace Dividend'.

I wish to express my thanks to the Public Relations Departments of the Defence Ministries of the NATO Alliance which supplied material for this volume and to the following individuals and companies for providing photographs: British Aerospace; Emerson Electric Company; Euromissile; FMC; Christopher F. Foss; Terry Gander; GKN Defence; Michel C. Klaver; Michael Ledford; OTO Melara; Panhard; Shorts; Pierre Touzin; Steven J. Zaloga; C. R. Zwart and my special thanks to Tim Neate for creating the line-drawings.

Simon Dunstan

2. A *Leopard Bergepanzer* demonstrates the lifting capacity of its front-mounted jib crane – a maximum of 20,000 kilograms when used in conjunction with the dozer blade as a stabilizer as shown here.

3. For many years Jeep-type vehicles have been used for scouting and liaison but on the modern battlefield they are too vulnerable. Accordingly the French Army has devised a light armoured vehicle or VBL (*Véhicule Blindé Léger*). Manufactured by Panhard, the VBL is used by the French Army in two basic versions: one armed with the Euromissile MILAN ATGW in the anti-tank role and one armed with machine-guns for scouting. This VBL is one of three bought off-the-shelf by the French Army in 1985 for use by its contingent in Lebanon.

4. The Saxon is issued to UK-based infantry battalions destined to reinforce the British Army of the Rhine (BAOR) in time of war. Here, Saxons, deployed from Britain, take part in Exercise 'Certain Strike' with GPMG 7.62mm machine-guns installed on the DISA mount forward of the commander's cupola.

5. There are a number of variants based on the Saxon including a recovery vehicle, seen here with its Hudson Wharton capstan hydraulic winch mounted on the side of the hull. This version has a four-man crew, in this case members of the Royal Electrical and Mechanical Engineers (REME).

6. The French equivalent of Saxon is the VAB (*Véhicule de l'Avant Blindé*) or Forward Area Armoured Vehicle. In its basic troop-carrying capacity, the VAB VTT (*Véhicule Transport de Troupe*) has a crew of two and carries ten fully equipped infantrymen.

7. Armed with a 7.62mm machine-gun in a *Creusot-Loire Industrie* CB.52 gun mounting, this VAB is fitted with the RATAC (*Radar de Tir pour Artillerie de Campagne*) fire control radar system for field artillery of the '155 AU FI' artillery regiments within armoured divisions. There is a 6×6 version of the VAB, currently in production for export, which bears a strong resemblance to the West German *Transportpanzer*.

8. The Véhicule Tracteur de Mortier or VTM 120 is a mortar-towing vehicle for the Thomson Brandt 120mm mortar, visible here on a railway flatcar. The VTM 120 has a crew of six and carries 70 mortar bombs. The French Army has a requirement for 4,430 VAB vehicles and variants for delivery by the early 1990s. (Pierre Touzin)

9. The VAB is a 4×4 vehicle and is fully amphibious, being propelled in water by two Dowty hydrojets. This version is the VAB RITA (Automatic Integrated Transmission Network) and normally has a crew of four. (Pierre Touzin)

9

10. There are several variants of the VAB in service with the French Army. This is a command post model or VB PC (*Poste de Commandement*), which is fitted with mapboards and additional communications equipment, with a crew of six. (Pierre Touzin)

11. For use by engineers, the VAB has been modified to carry specialized equipment, such as a rubber dinghy on the roof and is known as the VAB *Génie*. This model has a crew of nine and is armed with a *Creusot-Loire Industrie* CB 127 gunshield for the .50 calibre (12.7mm) M2 HB Browning machine-gun. (Pierre Touzin)

12. In the mid sixties, the Bundeswehr issued requirements for an 8×8 reconnaissance vehicle, 4×4 and 6×6 armoured load-carriers and a complete range of high-mobility 4×4, 6×6 and 8×8 tactical cargo trucks (see Fotofax *Nato Support Vehicles*). All these vehicles were to share many common components in order to reduce procurement costs. The 4×4 armoured load-carrier was known as the *Transportpanzer* 2 and the 6×6 version, as shown here, the *Transportpanzer* 1.

13. Manufactured by Thyssen Henschel, the *Transportpanzer* 1 is also called *Fuchs* (Fox). The vehicle is fully amphibious and propelled in water by two Schottel propellers at the rear of the hull. The rear compartment can be fitted with seats to carry ten infantrymen or a payload of 2,000 kilograms in the amphibious mode and 4,000 kilograms on land. It has a crew of two.

14. The *Fuchs* is produced in several versions for the West German Army including a Command and Communications variant as shown here. A total of 134 of this model have been built under the designation FüFu. Normal armament comprises a 7.62mm MG3 machine-gun above the commander's position. (Michel Klaver)

14

15. Other variants of the *Fuchs* include an NBC Reconnaissance model; an engineer vehicle; electronic warfare type TPz 1 Eloka; supply carrier and, illustrated here, a *Transportpanzer* 1 with the RASIT battlefield surveillance radar. This version is known in the Bundeswehr as the *Panzeraufklärungsradargerät* or PARA for short, and 110 are in service.

15

16. Numerous variants of the M113 remain in widespread service within NATO. The model illustrated is an M106 4.2in (107mm) Mortar Carrier of the Dutch Army. The M30 mortar is mounted on a turntable in the rear of the hull which allows a traverse of 43 degrees right and 46 degrees left. The 0.50in (12.7mm) M2 HB heavy machine-gun is retained at the commander's position.

17. The Bundeswehr also employs the M106 as a mortar-carrier but in a diesel-powered version designated M106A1. This model carries 88 mortar bombs as against 93 for the M106. Hidden beneath the camouflage is a mortar baseplate and bridge carried on the left side of the hull that allows the mortar to be fired dismounted from the vehicle, if required. (Pierre Touzin)

18. As its mortar-carrier, the French Army uses a variant of the AMX-10 Infantry Combat Vehicle. This model tows a 120mm Thomson-Brandt MO-120-RT-61 rifled mortar and carries 60 rounds of ammunition, under the designation AMX-10 TM or Mortar Tractor. The AMX-10 TM has a crew of six and is fitted with a Toucan 1 turret.

19. The armoured repair vehicle of the AMX-10 family is the AMX-10 ECH. With a crew of five including driver, commander and three mechanics, the ECH has a hydraulically-operated crane with an extending jib which can lift a maximum of 6,000 kilograms; here replacing the Hispano-Suiza engine of an AMX-10P ICV.

20. The FV434 Carrier, Maintenance, Full Tracked is used to undertake first-line repairs in the field. Manned by members of the Royal Electrical and Mechanical Engineers (REME), the FV434 is capable of changing the powerpack of a Chieftain MBT but not that of a Challenger.

21. The timely evacuation of casualties from the front line is essential to the maintenance of morale in modern armies. Armoured vehicles are necessary for this task and it is usual for a variant of the standard APC to be used. The US Army employs the M113A1 in this role. (Pierre Touzin)

22. An FV432 Ambulance of the 17th/21st Lancers passes the review stand at the conclusion of a field exercise. This model carries four stretcher patients or two stretcher and five seated patients, plus a crew of two.

23. The Dutch Army employs a variant of the YPR 765 Armoured Infantry Fighting Vehicle family as its front-line armoured ambulance. Designated the YPR 765 PRGWT, this model can carry four stretcher cases and seats are provided for two medical orderlies. (Pierre Touzin)

24. The Renault VAB *Sanitaire* (Ambulance) is in service with French Armed Forces. This version of the *Véhicule de l'Avant Blindé* has a roof-mounted air-conditioning system and can carry four stretcher or ten seated patients.

25. In accordance with the Geneva Convention, armoured ambulances display prominent red crosses and carry no armament. The Saxon Armoured Ambulance can carry four stretcher cases and one or two medical orderlies in addition to the commander and driver.

26. The M577A1 Command Post is an M113 variant with a higher superstructure than the basic APC for use as a command, communications or fire-control vehicle. Seen here is a fire-control vehicle of a howitzer battery of the 11th Armored Cavalry Regiment based at Fulda on the Inner German Border.

27. The first models of the M577 were completed in 1962 and were conversions of existing M113 APCs with plates extending from the original roofline. The weld seam along the side of this Italian M577 indicates that this is an early production model. It carries a rolled tent on the roof which can be erected to the rear to increase the usable working area.

28. Although the M577 is an efficient design, its very shape indicates that it is a command vehicle and therefore a priority target to the enemy. In consequence, some armies prefer to use a simpler conversion of the standard APC despite its much reduced working space such as this M113A1 command vehicle of the Canadian Mechanized Brigade Group in Germany.

29. The M548 Tracked Cargo Carrier uses many components of the standard M113 APC as a re-supply vehicle for forward units in the battle area. First produced in 1966, the M548 chassis forms the basis of various other weapon systems such as Tracked Rapier and the Lance tactical nuclear missile system.

30. The current production model of the Cargo Carrier is the M548A1 which incorporates improvements of the M113A2 APC. Here, an M548A1 of the US 2nd Armored Division acts as an ammunition re-supply vehicle to a field artillery unit during Exercise 'Crossed Swords' against I British Corps in 1986. Armed with a .50 calibre machine-gun, the M548 is fully amphibious and capable of carrying a maximum load of 5,443 kilograms. (C. R. Zwart)

31

32

31, 32. Mechanized bridgelayers are essential within a battlegroup in order to cross waterways and gulleys in the path of its intended line of movement. Rivers pose the greatest obstacle to mobility and an extending bridge system is one effective means of spanning narrower watercourses. Here, an AMX-13 Armoured Bridgelayer, designated MEKONG, demonstrates its hydraulic folding bridge which is 14.3m long and capable of carrying Class 25 vehicles. When two bridges are laid side by side, vehicles of up to Class 50, such as Main Battle Tanks, can be carried. The AMX-13 Bridgelayer has a crew of three: commander, driver and bridge operator.

33. The current US Army mechanized bridgelayer is the M60 AVLB (Armored Vehicle Launched Bridge) and approximately 1,100 AVLBs are in service, including a proportion based on the chassis of M48A5 gun tanks. The aluminium bridge is of the scissors type and is launched hydraulically over the front of the vehicle (an operation which takes approximately three minutes) to span gaps up to 18.3m wide. Other NATO users of the M48/60 AVLB include Spain and West Germany. (Michael Ledford)

34. The Bundeswehr also employs a bridgelayer designed and built by Mak of Kiel based on the Leopard 1 chassis. Its official designation is *Brückenlegepanzer Biber* or BRP-1; *Biber* being German for beaver.

34

35. The principal attribute of the *Biber* is its ability to extend its 22m aluminium bridge horizontally allowing a gap of up to 20m to be spanned. This is a distinct tactical advantage because it is far less likely to be detected from a distance than vertical AVLBs. The Bundeswehr introduced 105 Leopard *Biber* AVLBs into service. (Pierre Touzin)

36. Other NATO users of the Leopard Bridgelayer include Canada (6), Italy (64) and the Netherlands (25). Here, this bridgelayer is making its way through a German village during a tactical field exercise; the Maple Leaf insignia indicates that it is Canadian. The dozer blade on the front acts as a support during bridgelaying operations.

37. The British Army's AVLB is based on the chassis of the Chieftain MBT and is of two types: illustrated is the scissors-type No. 8 Tank Bridge. Operated by 32 Armoured Engineer Regiment, Royal Engineers, each AVLB has a crew of three and one No. 8 or No. 9 Tank Bridge with the other being carried on a special semi-trailer towed by a Scammell Crusader prime mover.

38. In order to achieve greater versatility and to reduce procurement and operating costs, it is common practice to design a range of vehicles based on the chassis of the current MBT. Typical of this concept is the Leopard 1 family illustrated here, with, from right to left: Leopard 1A1A1; Leopard Armoured Recovery Vehicle (ARV); Leopard Armoured Engineer Vehicle (AEV) and Leopard Bridgelayer.

38

39. First produced by Mak of Kiel in 1966, the Leopard ARV, or *Bergepanzer* (BPZ) as it is designated in the Bundeswehr, has been designed to recover battle-damaged or broken-down AFVs from the battlefield and to change major assemblies in the field. Here, a *Bergepanzer* demonstrates its lifting capability to a maximum of 20,000 kilograms. Note the triple deep-fording snorkel tubes in the foreground beside the Leopard 1 MBT.

40. A Leopard *Bergepanzer* recovers a bogged-down MBT by means of its front-mounted hydraulic winch which has a pulling capacity of 35,000 kilograms (70,000kg with appropriate tackle). Armament of the BPZ is one 7.62mm MG3 on the commander's cupola and another mounted in the hull front. The Bundeswehr has procured 544 Leopard *Bergepanzers* of which 104 BPZs are currently being converted to become *Pionierpanzer* 2 AEVs.

41. In past conflicts, many AFVs have been lost because of mechanical defects or minor battle-damage. In consequence, one of the principal roles of the ARV is to undertake battlefield repair of stranded AFVs by replacing components up to and including complete powerpacks; on the Leopard *Bergepanzer* a spare powerpack can be carried on its rear deck for immediate replacement. Here, a *Bergepanzer* changes the powerpack of a Leopard 1A3; the fastest recorded Leopard engine change from the tank stopping to moving off again is eight minutes!

42. Due to the widespread sale of Leopard 1 MBTs within NATO, the ARV is in service with Belgium (36); Canada (eight) – under the name Taurus; Greece (four); Italy (69); Netherlands (52); Norway (six) and Turkey (four) as well as the Bundeswehr. This example in travelling configuration is in service with the Royal Netherlands Army. (Michel Klaver)

42

43. The FV4204 Chieftain Mark 5 ARV is currently the standard heavy tracked recovery vehicle of the British Army. This ARV is shown in travelling order with a tarpaulin over the rear decks as living and working quarters for the four-man crew of Royal Electrical and Mechanical Engineers. The Chieftain entered service with the British Army in 1976, and a total of 257 was produced up until 1980.

44. The fleet of British Army Chieftain ARVs has recently been modified with the addition of a hydraulic crane on the left rear side in order to be able to lift the powerpack of the Challenger MBT. This vehicle is designated Chieftain Mark 7 Armoured Repair and Recovery Vehicle (ARRV); an example is shown here dismounting from a Scammell Commander tank-transporter.

45. Despite this modification, the Chieftain ARRV is unable to support fully the Challenger MBT regiments in BAOR. As a result, a Challenger Armoured Repair and Recovery Vehicle or CRAAV is currently in production with thirty vehicles being built at present; illustrated is the first of six pre-production examples built by Vickers Defence Systems at their Armstrong Works.

46. The *Char de Dépannage* AMX Model 55 is the standard light tracked ARV of the French Army and is based on the chassis of the AMX-13 light tank. Manufactured by Creusot-Loire Industrie of Chalon-sur-Saône, the AMX Model 55 is powered by a SOFAM 250hp petrol engine or latterly by a GM Detroit Diesel unit of 280hp. Armament is a single 7.62mm machine-gun at the commander's cupola.

45

46

47. The AMX Model 55 is fitted with an A-frame hoist which can lift components such as an AMX-13 gun turret or a maximum weight of 5,000 kilograms to a height of 3.4 metres. The vehicle has two winches with a maximum capacity of 17,000 kilograms and the recovery of stranded vehicles is effected to the rear.

48. The ARV version of the current French Army MBT is the AMX-30D or *Char* AMX-30 *Dépanneur-Niveleur*. With a crew of four comprising commander, driver and two mechanics, the ARV is based on the standard AMX-30 chassis with an armoured superstructure housing the crew and the main recovery winch. At the front of the hull is a hydraulically operated dozer blade to stabilize the vehicle during winching operations.

49. The AMX-30D embodies a Griffet crane for changing major AFV assemblies. It can lift a load of 12,000 kilograms through 240 degrees, or a maximum of 15,000 kilograms such as the turret of an MBT, when the crane is facing towards the front and with the dozer blade lowered. Here, an AMX-30D removes the powerpack of an AMX-30 having towed it to a sheltered spot by means of A-frame bars.

50. The AMX-30D can snorkel to a depth of four metres and is provided with an NBC system as well as numerous recovery and repair tools on the exterior of the vehicle including a Retel TRA251 auxiliary winch on the hull front with a capacity of 3,500 kilograms for recovering light vehicles and for deploying the heavy main winch rope.

48

49

50

51. A total of 134 AMX-30D ARVs are in service with the French Army, and other NATO users include Greece and Spain. In common with many ARV designs, a spare powerpack is carried on the rear of the hull (here covered by a tarpaulin) for the rapid replacement of a defective engine in the field.

52. The standard ARV in the US Army remains the M88 which has been in service since 1961. By 1964, when production ceased, 1,075 M88s had been built but, due to an urgent requirement for more recovery vehicles for the US Army, the line was reopened in 1975 for the manufacture of an improved version powered by a variant of the diesel engine used in the M60 MBT. A total of 878 of the earlier model were also modified to the same standard which was type classified as the M88A1.

53. Manufactured by BMY of York, Pennsylvania, 2,167 M88A1s were built before production ended in early 1989. Other NATO users of the M88 include Greece, Norway, Portugal, Spain and West Germany. An improved version known as the M88A1E1 (or M88A2 when type classified) has been developed to support the M1 and M1A1 Abrams MBT.

54. An M88A1 Medium Recovery Vehicle named Desert Fox tows an Oshkosh M911 (8×6) truck trailer to the repair site of the 26th Supply Service Company area during a 'Reforger' exercise in Germany; a simple task for this powerful vehicle. A total of 2,470 M88 ARVs remain in service with the US Army.

55. Designed for hoisting, winching and towing operations to effect battlefield recovery and repair, an M88A1 demonstrates its A-frame boom to lift upright an M113A1 APC. With the stabilizing blade lowered and its suspension locked out, the M88A1 can lift a load up to 22,680 kilograms. Standard armament is a single .50 calibre Browning machine-gun. (Steven Zaloga)

56

56. Another variant based on the AMX-13 light tank is the *Véhicule de Combat du Génie* (VCG) or AMX-13 Engineer Combat Vehicle. The VCG has been designed to undertake a variety of roles on the battlefield and can tow a four-wheel trailer (as illustrated) carrying additional engineer stores such as demolition charges.

57. At the front of the vehicle is a hydraulically operated dozer blade which can excavate 45 cubic metres of soil per hour as well as clearing battlefield obstacles. The VCG has a crew of two, commander and driver who operates the dozer blade, and can carry up to seven combat engineers in the rear hull.

58. Armed with a single .50 calibre M2HB machine-gun, the VCG is provided with an A-frame boom which can lift a maximum load of 4,500 kilograms by means of a drum winch mounted externally on the front of the superstructure. Here, a VCG ROCROI places a fascine with its A-frame boom to form a bridge across a stream.

59. The FV180 Combat Engineer Tractor entered service with the British Army in 1978. It has been designed for use by Sappers of the Royal Engineers in the combat zone in support of the battle group in both offensive and defensive operations. A total of 141 CETs have been built for the British Army.

60

60. Constructed of all-welded aluminium armour, the principal role of the CET is to undertake digging tasks with its large-capacity dozer bucket which is capable of moving 200 cubic metres of soil per hour over a hauling distance of 100 metres. The vehicle has a crew of two and can be driven in either direction with equal ease, although the bucket is at the rear.

61. Weighing 18 tonnes, the CET is fully amphibious with a minimum of preparation and is propelled in water by two Dowty hydrojets. The CET can tow various engineer trailers as well as carry and launch Class 30 and Class 60 trackway or the 'Maxi-Pipe' fascine normally carried by AVREs. Other equipments include a pusher bar for launching bridging pontoons and a jib crane for handling palletized stores.

61

62

62. The Royal Engineers also use a variant of the FV432 APC fitted with specialized engineer equipment such as that shown here. On the top of the APC is a THORN EMI Ranger scatterable mine system. It comprises 72 tubes, each containing eighteen anti-personnel mines, which can be fired to a range of 100 metres forming a random pattern on the ground at a rate of eighteen mines per second. The vehicle is also towing a Bar minelayer which is capable of burying anti-tank mines at a rate of up to 600 mines per hour.

63. Pending the introduction of a purpose-designed Armoured Vehicle Royal Engineers (AVRE), the British Army of the Rhine (BAOR) has converted a number of Chieftain MBTs to Armoured Engineer Vehicles (AEV) capable of carrying a variety of engineer stores, such as Class 60 trackway and 'Maxi-Pipe' fascines as shown here, and either a dozer blade or mineploughs (as illustrated). With a three-man crew, it can also tow all current combat engineer trailers carrying additional stores. (Terry Gander)

64. Until such time as there are sufficient Chieftain ARVEs, the venerable Centurion AVRE will continue in service. It comes in two versions, one armed with a 165mm demolition gun and the other armed with the standard L7 105mm tank gun firing HESH rounds only. Here, a Centurion AVRE 105 is fitted with a Pearson Engineering Mine Plough and tows Giant Viper anti-tank mine-clearing equipment.

65. Based on the M60A1 MBT, the M728 Combat Engineer Vehicle (CEV) has been designed to undertake numerous engineer tasks on the battlefield including the destruction of field fortifications such as pillboxes and strong points with its M135 165mm demolition gun for which 30 rounds of ammunition are carried. This M728 CEV is taking part in the Allied Armed Forces Day parade in Berlin.

66. The M728 CEV is issued to Engineer Battalions within armoured, mechanized and infantry divisions with eight in engineer battalions of armoured and mechanized divisions and three in infantry division engineer battalions. Separate engineer companies have two M728 CEVs each. With a large-capacity, front-mounted dozer blade, the CEV is fitted with an A-frame boom which has a maximum lifting capacity of 15,876 kilograms.

67. In 1958 the US Army began development of a vehicle called the All-purpose Ballastable Crawler (ABC) which subsequently became known as the Universal Engineer Tractor (UET). Prototypes were built by the Caterpillar Tractor Company and the International Harvester Company. This vehicle was type classified as the M9 Armoured Engineer Earthmover (ACE) in 1977. BMY is currently building 566 M9 ACEs, the first production models having been delivered in late 1989, more than 30 years after development work began!

68

69

68. A sister vehicle to the Leopard *Bergepanzer* or ARV is the *Pionierpanzer* or AEV which differs in detail for the armoured engineer role. While the AEV can fulfil most of the tasks of the ARV, the *Pionierpanzer* carries an earth auger in place of a spare powerpack on the rear hull. This device is used for digging holes for demolition charges, foxholes or for foundations. The Bundeswehr has 36 Leopard AEVs and other NATO users include Belgium (six), Italy (40 – of which 28 were built by OTO Melara) and the Netherlands (28).

69. The other major difference of the Leopard *Pionierpanzer* is the larger dozer blade with the installation of a heat-exchanger which allows almost continuous dozing operations without overheating; the blade can also be fitted with four scarifiers for ripping up the surface of roads to impede enemy movement. All the West German Leopard AEVs are currently being converted to become *Pionierpanzer* 2.

70. The *Pionierpanzer* 2 or *Dachs* (Badger) is very similar to the AEV but features a telescopic excavator arm in place of the jib crane, with an earth working capacity of 140 cubic metres an hour. The Bundeswehr has a requirement for 140 *Dachs* while the Canadian Army has placed an order for nine.

71. Based on the same chassis as the M107 and M110 self-propelled guns, the M578 is a light ARV designed to support artillery units equipped with the aforementioned weapons. It is in widespread NATO service including the armies of Canada; Denmark; Netherlands; Norway; Spain; UK and the USA. This M578, CONDOR, belongs to the Dutch Army.

72

73

72. A pair of 105mm Mk 61 self-propelled howitzers takes up fire positions during a field exercise. Based on the AMX-13 light tank chassis, its full designation is *Obusier de 105 Modèle 50 sur Affût Automoteur* and it has been in service with the French Army since 1958.

73. With a fixed fighting compartment at the rear, the 105mm M1950 howitzer has a traverse of 20 degrees left and right and 56 rounds of ammunition are carried. Although superseded by the 155 AU FI in armoured and mechanized divisions, the Mk 61 remains in service in support of infantry formations.

74. The crew of a 155mm self-propelled gun Mk F3 ram home a projectile during gunnery practice. Designated the *Canon de 155mm Mk F3 Automoteur* (C-155-F3-Am), it is another variant of the AMX-13 family. More than 600 Mk F3 SPGs have been produced with 222 for the French Army.

75. A 155 AU FI self-propelled gun displays the 66 degrees maximum elevation of its 155mm ordnance during training on a French Army firing range. The 155 AU FI is deployed in artillery regiments of four batteries with five SPGs in each battery.

76

77

76. Originally called the 155mm GCT or *Grand Cadence de Tir* (High Rate of Fire), the 155 AU FI incorporates an automatic loading system, and 42 rounds of separate ammunition are carried in the rear of the turret which can be reloaded by a crew of four in fifteen minutes with the turret rear folding horizontal (as shown) to form a working platform.

77. The automatic loading system allows a sustained rate of fire of eight rounds a minute – two to three rounds a minute with manual loading should the system fail. The gunner can select single shots or bursts of six rounds which can be fired within 45 seconds for saturation bombardment of a target. The French Army has a requirement for 190 155 AU FI systems.

78. One of the most successful instances of weapons standardization within NATO is that of the M109 155mm Self-propelled Howitzer – of NATO's sixteen nations, twelve employ the system. The example illustrated is an improved version produced by OTO Melara featuring a long barrel capable of firing existing M107 rounds as well as FH-70 ammunition.

	AMX-10P (France)	Marder (Germany)	VCC-80 (Italy)	AIFV (Belgium/ Netherlands)
Crew	3 + 8	9	3 + 6	3 + 7
Combat Weight	14500kg	29207kg	19000kg	13687kg
Hull Length	5.778m	6.79m	6.705m	5.258m
Width	2.78m	3.24m	3.0m	2.819m
Hull Roof Height	1.92m	1.9m	1.75m	2.007m
Overall Height	2.57m	2.985m	2.6m	2.794m
Max. Road Speed	65km/h	75km/h	70km/h	61.2km/h
Max. Water Speed	7km/h	—	—	6.3km/h
Fuel Capacity	528 litres	652 litres	—	416 litres
Max. Road Range	600km	520km	600km	490km
Gradient	60%	60%	60%	60%
Side Slope	30%	30%	40%	30%
Vertical Obstacle	0.7m	1m	0.85m	0.635m
Trench	2.1m	2.5m	2.5m	1.625m
Engine	Hispano-Suiza HS-115 V-8 water-cooled super-charged diesel of 300hp	MTU MB 833 Ea-500 6-cylinder liquid-cooled diesel of 600hp	FIAT V-6 turbo-charged inter-cooled diesel of 480hp	Detroit Diesel 6V-53 V-6 liquid-cooled diesel of 264hp
Transmission	Pre-selective with 4 forward and 1 reverse gears	4-speed HSWL-194 planetary, 4 forward and 2 reverse gears with integral steering and braking system	ZF 20 HST 500 automatic	Allison TX100-1A automatic with 3 forward and 1 reverse gears
Steering			hydrostatic	FMC DS 200 mechanically controlled differential & pivot star
Suspension	Torsion bar	Torsion bar	Torsion bar	Torsion bar in tube
Armament, Main	1 × 20mm cannon	1 × 20mm cannon	1 × 25mm cannon	1 × 25mm cannon
Coaxial	1 × 7.62m MG	MILAN ATGW	1 × 7.62mm MG	1 × 7.62mm MG
Anti-aircraft	1 × 7.62mm or 12.7mm MG	1 × 7.62mm MG	1 × 7.62mm cannon	—
Ammunition, main	760	1250	400	180 ready + 144 reserve
Coaxial	2000	5000	1200	230 ready + 1610 reserve
	7.62mm 3200 12.7mm or 1000			
A/A	—	—	—	—
Smoke Laying Equipment	2 × 2 smoke dischargers	6 × smoke dischargers	2 × 3 smoke dischargers	6 × smoke dischargers
Power-to-Weight Ratio	20.68hp/tonne	20.54hp/tonne	25hp/tonne	19.29hp/tonne

	Warrior (UK)	**M113A2** (USA)	**M2 BRADLEY** (USA)
Crew	3 + 7	2 + 11	3 + 7
Combat Weight	24500kg	11341kg	22590kg
Hull Length	6.34m	4.863m	6.453m
Width	3.034m	2.686m	3.2m
Hull Roof Height	1.93m	1.85m	2.565m
Overall Height	2.791m	2.52m	2.972m
Max. Road Speed	82km/h	64.37km/h	66km/h
Max. Water Speed	—	5.8km/h	7.2km/h
Fuel Capacity	770 litres	360 litres	662 litres
Max. Road Range	660km	483km	483km
Gradient	60%	60%	60%
Side Slope	40%	30%	40%
Vertical Obstacle	0.75m	0.61m	0.914m
Trench	2.5m	1.68m	2.54m
Engine	Perkins Engines CV8 TCA V-8 diesel of 550hp	GMC Detroit Diesel model 6V-53 6-cylinder water-cooled diesel of 215hp	Cummins VTA-903T turbo- charged 8-cylinder diesel of 500hp
Transmission	Detroit Diesel Allison X-300-4B fully automatic 4 forward, 2 reverse gears differential steering	GMC Allison TX-100-1 with 3 forward and 1 reverse	General Electric HMPT500 hydro mechanical with hydro static steering
Steering	variable hydrostatic drive		
Suspension	Torsion bar	Torsion bar	Torsion bar
Armament, Main	1 × 30mm cannon	—	1 × 25mm cannon
	1 × 7.62mm Chain Gun	1 × 12.7mm MG	—
Coaxial	—	—	(1 × 7.62mm MG
Anti-aircraft			(2-Tube Tow launcher
			300 ready, 600 reserve
Ammunition, main	—	—	
Coaxial			800 ready, 1540 reserve
	—	2000	
	—	—	—
A/A	2 × 4 smoke		2 × 4 smoke
Smoke Laying	dischargers		dischargers plus
Equipment			exhaust generator
Power-to-Weight Ratio	22.45hp/tonne	18.51hp/tonne	20.38hp/tonne

79. In addition to its powerful armament and armour protection, Warrior has excellent mobility thanks to a high power-to-weight ratio of 22.45bhp/tonne derived from the Perkins Engines CV8 TCA 550hp diesel and Detroit Diesel Allison X-300-4B automatic transmission. Here, a pair of Warrior section vehicles advance under simulated fire during an exercise on Salisbury Plain.

Grizzly (Armoured Personnel

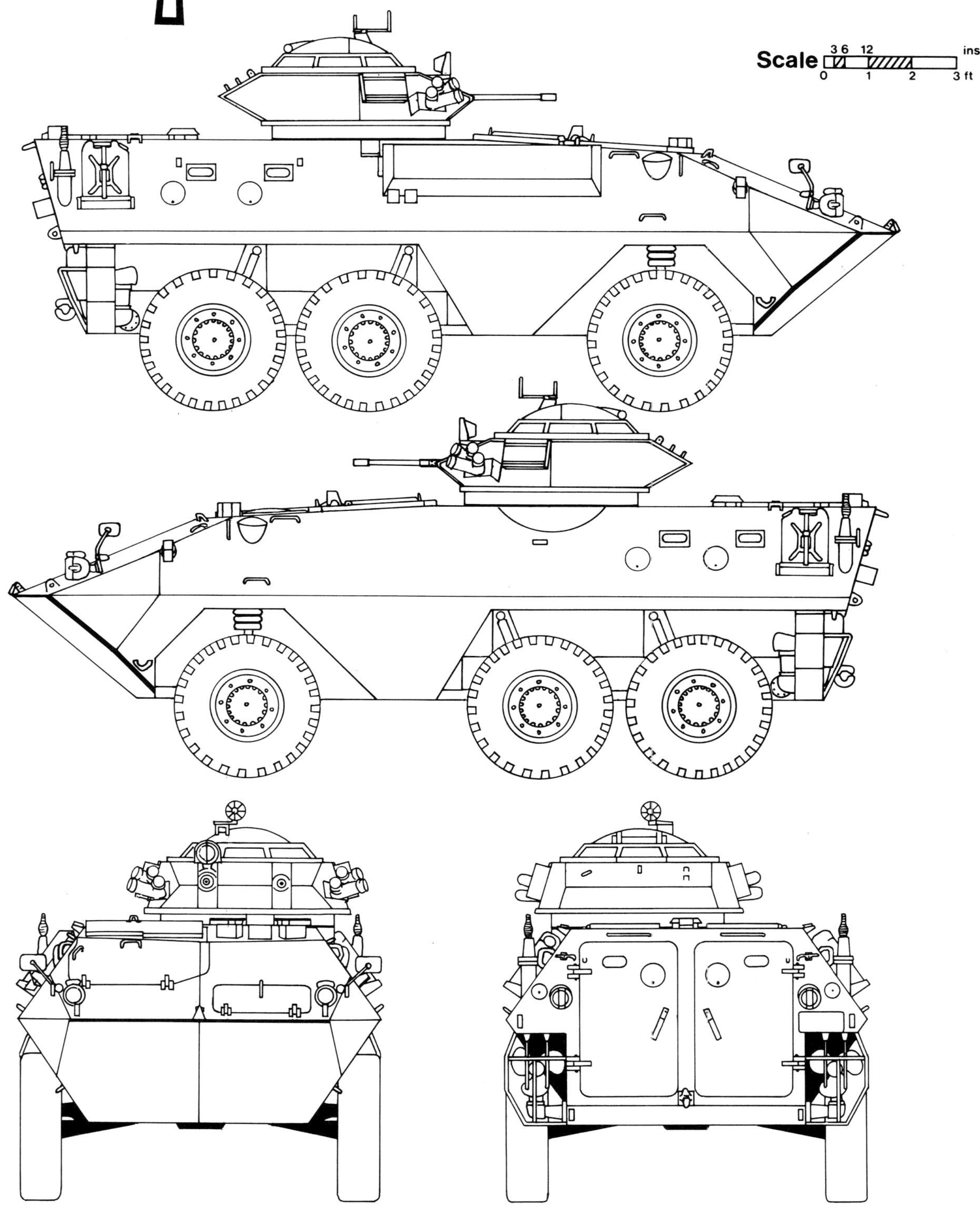

Carrier) Drawn by Tim Neate

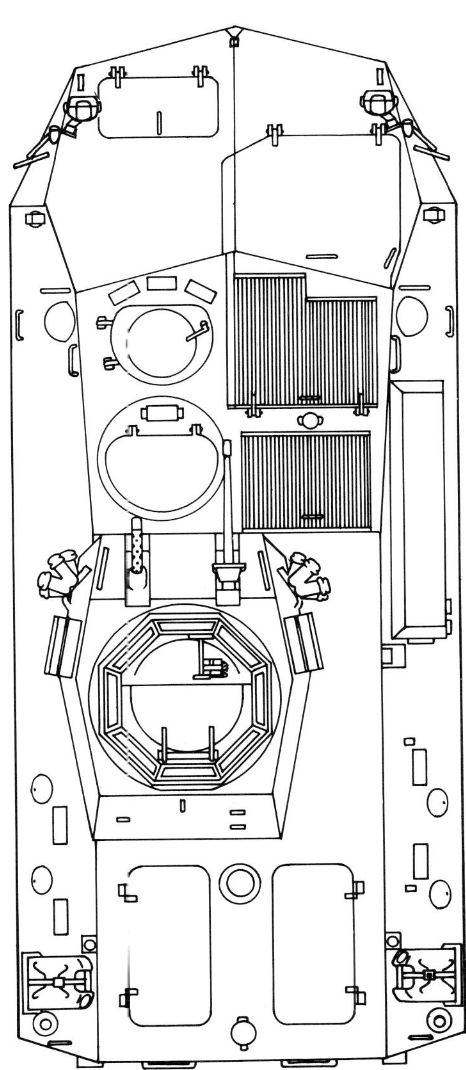

	GRIZZLY (Canada)
Crew	3 + 6
Combat Weight	10500kg
Hull Length	5.968m
Width	2.53m
Hull Roof Height	1.85m
Overall Height	2.53m
Max. Road Speed	101.5km/h
Max. Water Speed	7km/h
Fuel Capacity	204 litres
Max. Road Range	603km
Gradient	60%
Side Slope	30%
Vertical Obstacle	0.508m
Trench	0.406m
Engine	GM Detroit Diesel 6V-53T, 6-cylinder diesel of 215hp
Transmission	Allison MT-650 automatic, 5 forward and 1 reverse gears
Steering	Power assisted, front wheels
Suspension	Independent on all wheels
Armament, Main	1 × 12.7mm HB MG
Coaxial	1 × 7.62mm C5A1 GPMG
Anti-aircraft	—
Ammunition, main	12.7mm 1000
Coaxial	7.62mm 4400
A/A	—
Smoke Laying Equipment	2 × 4 No. 12 Mk 1 smoke dischargers
Power-to-Weight Ratio	

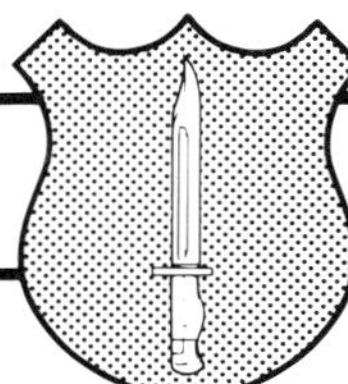

Saxon APC (Battlefield Taxi) Drawn by

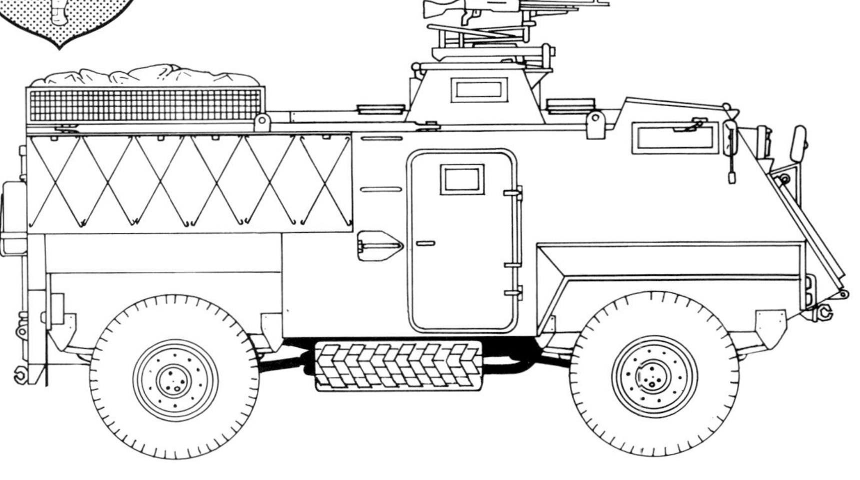

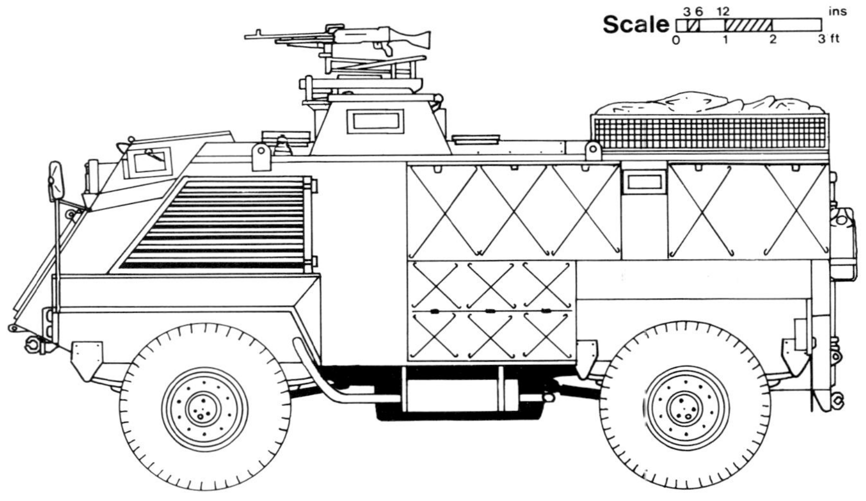

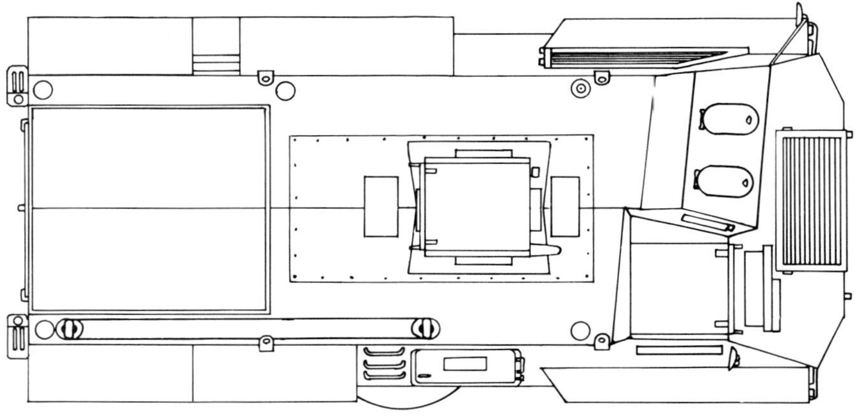

SAXON ARMOURED PERSONNEL CARRIER (UK)

Crew:	2 + 10
Combat Weight:	11660kg
Unloaded Weight:	9940kg
Length:	5.169m
Width:	2.489m
Height:	2.86m
Ground Clearance:	hull 0.41m; axles 0.29m
Wheelbase:	3.073m
Maximum speed:	96km/h
Fuel capacity:	153 litres
Maximum range:	480 km
Gradient:	60%
Fording:	1.12m
Turning radius:	7.57m
Engine:	Bedford 500 6-cylinder diesel developing 164 bhp at 2,800 rpm (alternatively; Perkins T6.3544 diesel developing 195 bhp at 2,500 rpm)
Powerto-weight ratio:	14.06 bhp/tonne
Transmission:	Allison AT-545 automatic with 4 forward and 1 reverse gears
Transfer case:	2-speed
Steering:	Burman, power-assisted
Suspension:	semi-elliptical springs and hydraulic shock absorbers
Tyres:	12.00 × 20, 13.00 × 20 or 14.00 × 20
Brakes:	main; drum, air/hydraulic (dual circuit)
Electrical system:	24V
Batteries:	2 × 12v, 100 Ah
Armour:	proof against 7.62mm AP rounds at point-blank range
Status:	In production and in service with Bahrain, Kuwait, Malaysia, Nigeria, Oman, United Arab Emirates and the British Army, both Regular and Territorial.
Manufacturer:	GKN Defence, Telford, Shropshire

Variants:

Saxon Command Vehicle: modified interior for use as a command post with extra radios; teleprinter and mapboards. This variant is in service with the Royal Artillery as a command post vehicle with Rapier SAM units.

Saxon Armoured Ambulance: modified interior to accommodate four NATO standard stretchers; medical equipment and one or two medical orderlies. In service with the Royal Army Medical Corps.

Saxon Recovery Vehicle: modified for use by four recovery mechanics with a side-mounted Hudson Wharton capstan 5,000kg hydraulic winch which can recover vehicles weighing up to 16,000kg with the use of block and tackle. In service with the Royal Electrical and Mechanical Engineers.

Saxon Internal Security Vehicles: there are several IS versions of Saxon including one mounting a one-man turret fitted with the ARWEN 37V rapid fire anti-riot weapon while another has a turret-mounted water cannon which can deliver 341 litres per minutes at high pressure capable of knocking down rioters at 15m.

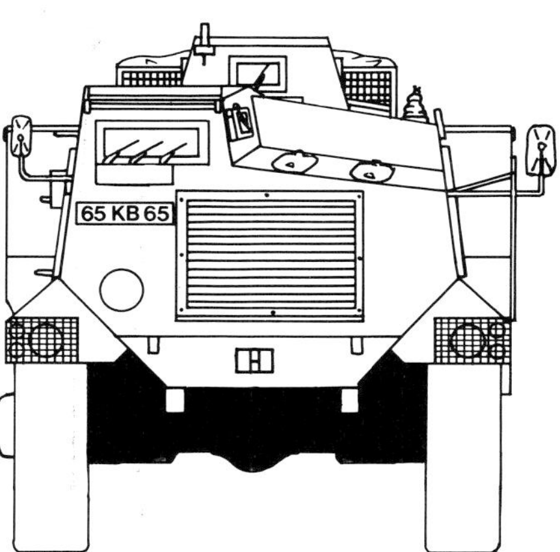

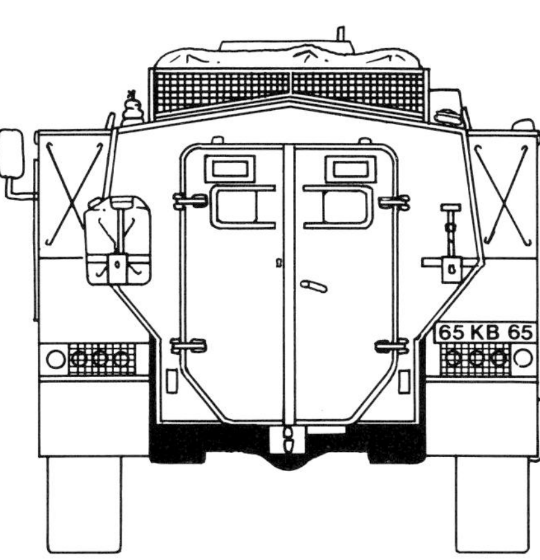

YPR-765 PRI (AIFV) Drawn by Tim Neate

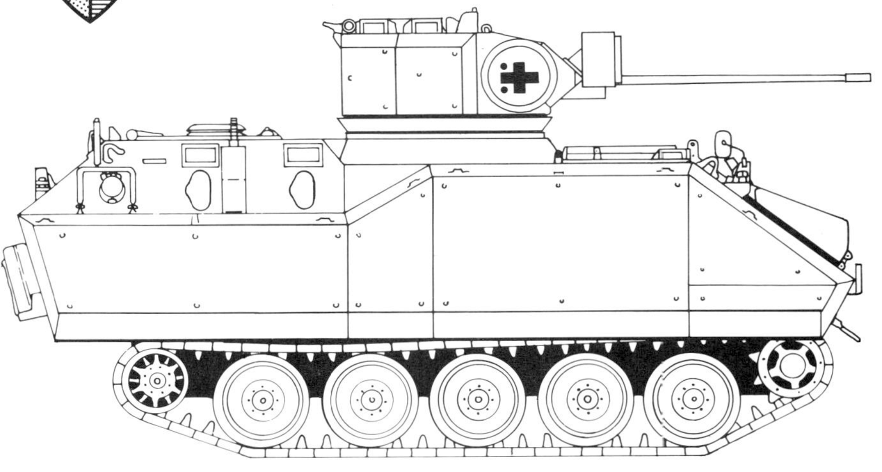

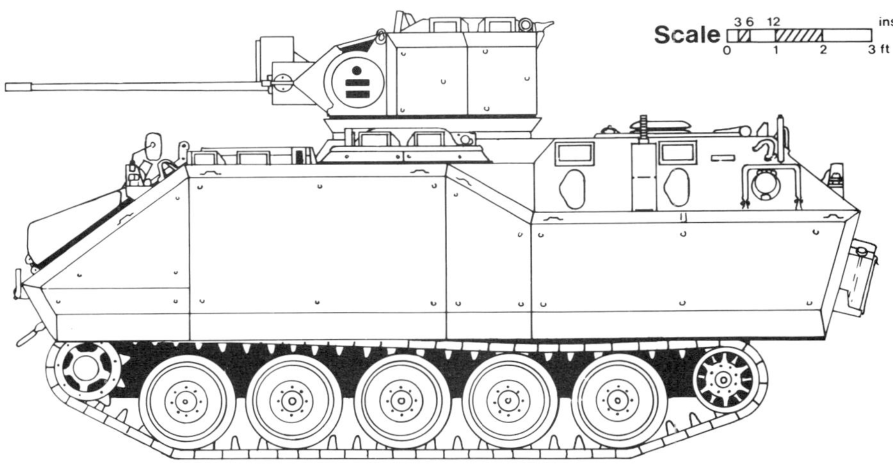

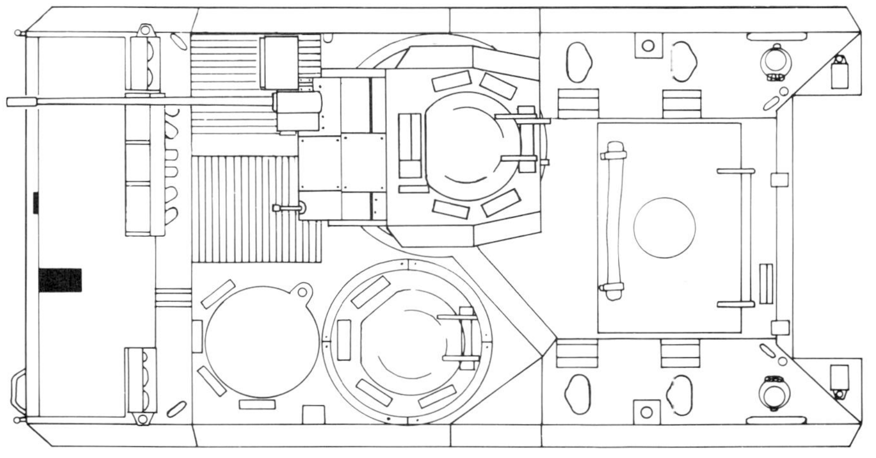

ARMORED INFANTRY FIGHTING VEHICLE

Crew	3 + 7
Combat Weight:	13687kg
Unloaded Weight:	11405kg
Length:	5.258m
Width:	2.819m
Height:	2.794m
Firing Height:	2.33m
Width over Tracks:	2.54m
Track Width:	0.381m
Ground Pressure:	0.67kg/cm^2
Ground Clearance:	0.432m
Fuel capacity:	416 litres
Maximum range:	490 km
Maximum speed:	road 62.2 km/h water 6.3 km/h
Acceleration:	0 to 32 km/h 10 seconds 0 to 48 km/h 23.1 seconds
Vertical obstacle:	0.635m
Trench:	1.625m
Gradient:	60%
Side slope:	30%
Turning radius:	7.62m
Engine:	Detroit Diesel 6V-53T V-6 liquid-cooled diesel developing 264 hp at 2800 rpm
Transmission and steering:	Allison TX100-1A automatic with 3 forward and 1 reverse gears. FMC DS 200 mechanically controlled differential and pivot steering.
Suspension:	torsion bar in tube
Electrical system:	28V
Batteries:	2 × 12V6TN
Armament:	main 1 × 25mm Oerlikon KBA-BO2 cannon coaxial, 1 × 7.62mm MG
Ammunition:	25mm 180 ready + 144 reserve 7.62mm 230 ready + 1610 reserve
Status:	In service with Belgium (514); Netherlands (1720) and Philippines (45). In production for the Turkish Army.
Manufacturer:	FMC Corporation, Ground Systems Division, Santa Clara, California. BMF Belgian Mechanical Fabrication, Seraing, Belgium, DAF, Eindhoven, Netherlands.

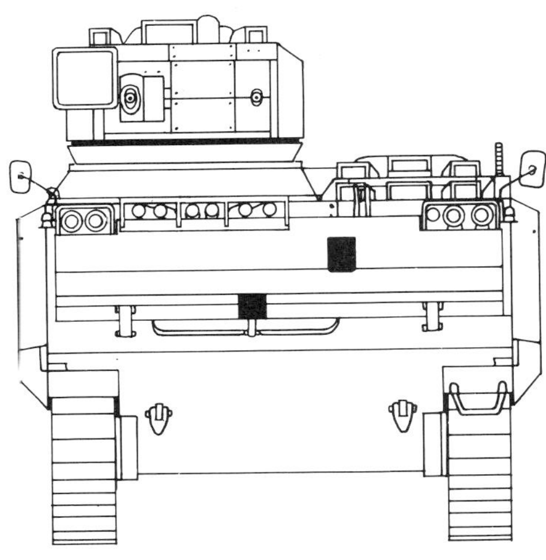

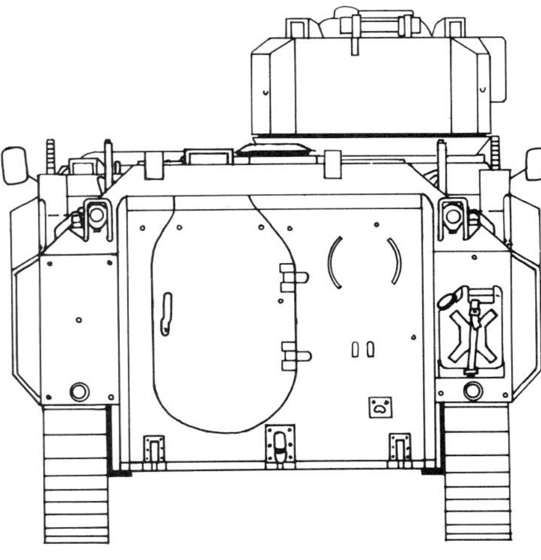

YPR-765 PRCO-C1 (Command

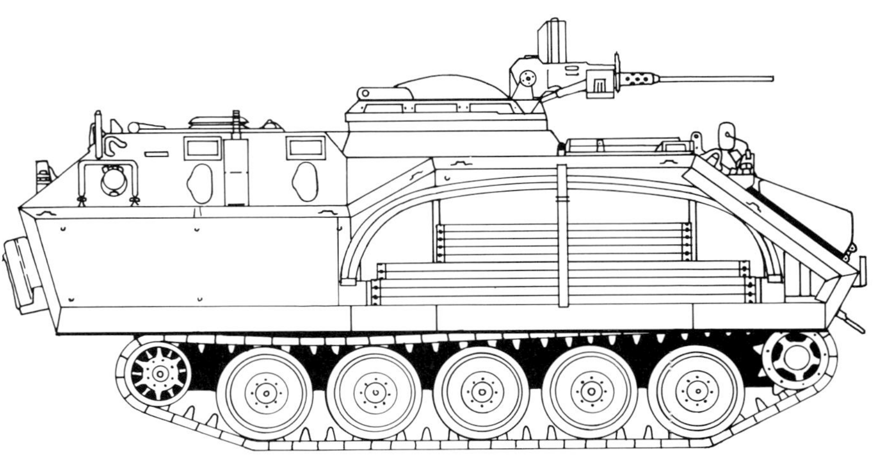

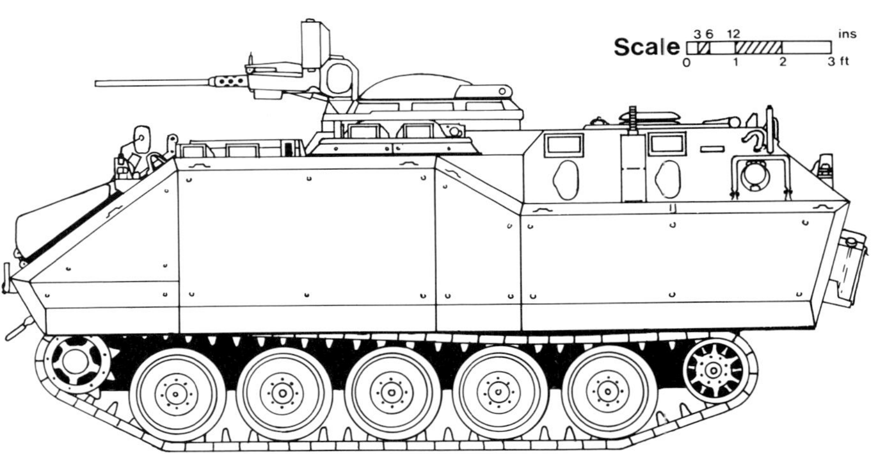

AIFV Variants:

Command Post: modified interior to accommodate a command staff of six plus its crew of three (commander, gunner and driver), and additional communications equipment; table & mapboards. It is normally fitted with a cupola mounting a 12.7mm (0.50in) M2 HB machine gun.

Mortar Prime Mover: tows a 120mm Thomson Brandt or similar mortar and has racks in the rear compartment for 51 mortar bombs. A crew of seven is carried with three vehicle crew and four mortar crew. It is normally armed with a 12.7mm machine-gun.

TOW ATGW Vehicle: a model fitted with the Emerson Electric Co ITV (Improved TOW Vehicle) kit or other types of ATGW systems such as HOT.

Cargo Carrier: with a crew of two, this model can carry up to 2040kg of cargo and the armament consists of a 12.7mm (0.50 in) M2 HB machine-gun.

Ambulance: modified interior to accommodate four stretchers suspended from hangars and two seats for medical orderlies. This model is unarmed.

Recovery Vehicle: fitted with a HIAB crane on the roof; additional buoyancy pods on the sides and front; and smoke dischargers mounted on the hull front.

ehicle) Drawn by Tim Neate

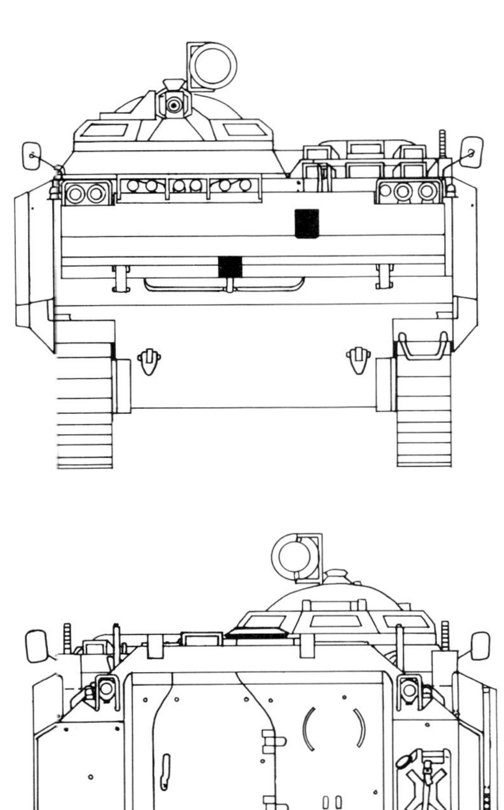

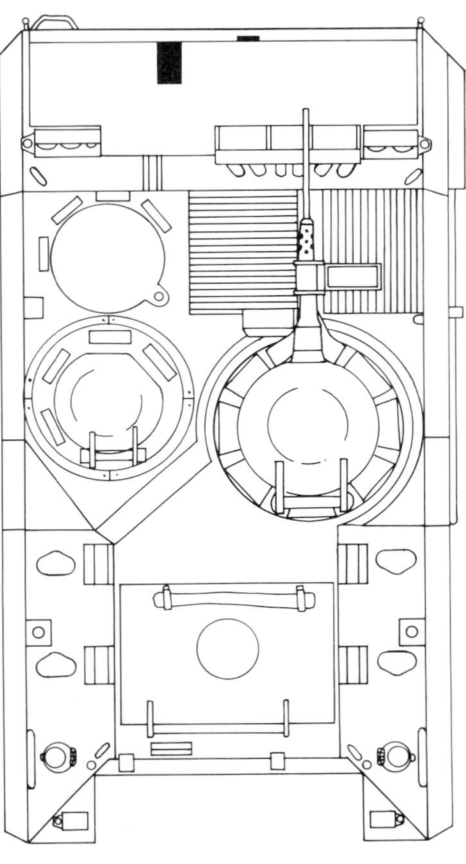

YPR-765 PRAT (TOW Vehicle) Draw

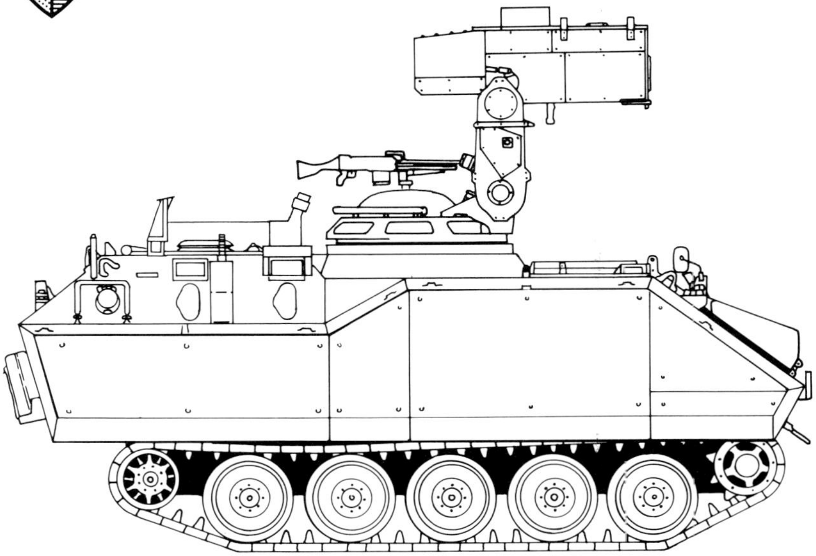

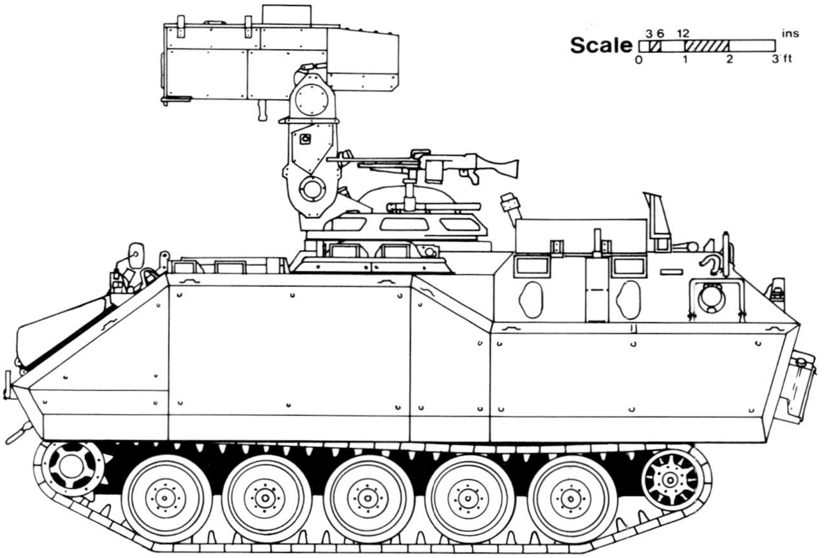

Netherlands Models:

In the Dutch Army, the AIFV is designated the YPR 765 PRI and other variants in service are:–

YPR 765 PRCO-B command vehicle, crew nine, combat weight 13,700kg.

YPR 765 PRCO-C1 to C5, crew nine, combat weight 12,400kg, armed with 12.7mm (0.50) M2 machine-gun. The C1 is a battalion commander's vehicle, C2 a battalion gunnery centre, C3 a mortar fire-control vehicle, C4 an AA command vehicle and C5 an observation vehicle with a crew of four. All these versions have an M113 type cupola with a 12.7mm M2 HB pintle-mounted machine gun.

YPR 765 PRRDR radar vehicle fitted with the British ZB 298 battlefield surveillance radar.

YPR 765 PRRDR-C radar/command vehicle

YPR 765 PRGWT ambulance, crew four, weight 11,600kg, unarmed.

YPR 765 PRI/I squad vehicle fitted with M113 type

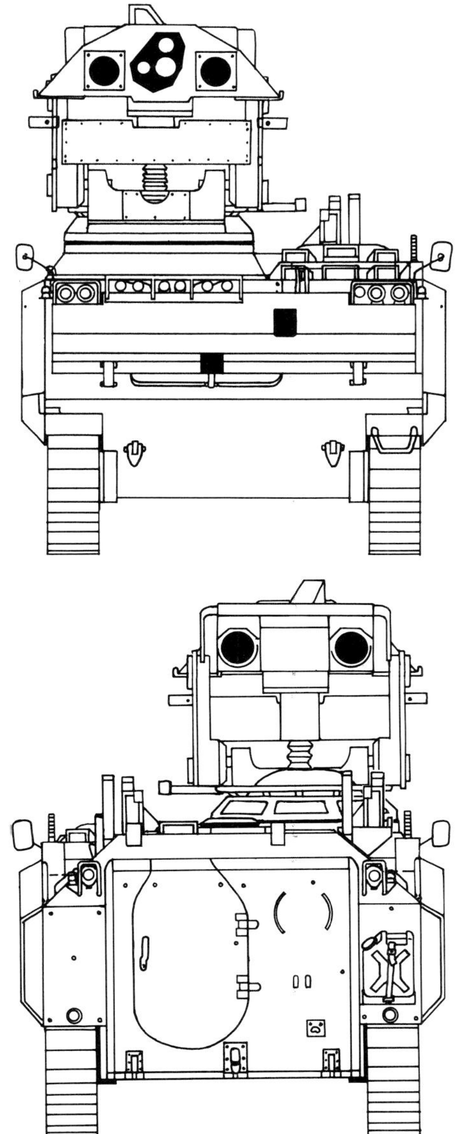

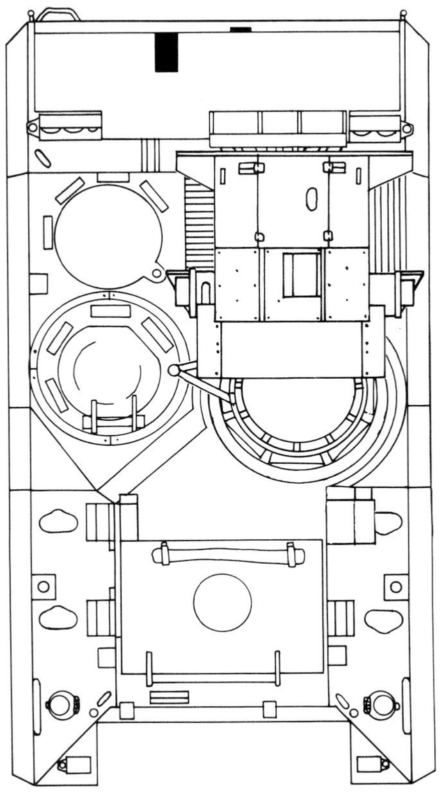

cupola with 12.7mm (0.50) M2 machine-gun, carries nine men plus driver.

YPR PRMR mortar tractor (tows 120mm Thomson Brandt mortar), crew seven, combat weight 13,000kg, armament one 12.7mm (0.50) M2 machine-gun pintle-mounted on a standard M113 type cupola.

YPR 765 PRVR-A and PRVR-B cargo vehicles, crew two, combat weight 13,400kg, armament one 12.7mm (0.50) M2 machine-gun pintle-mounted on a standard M113 type cupola.

YPR 765 PRAT fitted with the Emerson TOW launcher system as fitted to the M901 Improved TOW Vehicle.

YPR 806 PRBRG armoured recovery vehicle, crew four, weight 12,200kg, armament one 12.7mm (0.50) M2 machine gun.

80

80. Among the numerous schemes to extend the life of the M109 series is the HIP or Howitzer Improvement Program proposed by the US Army in conjunction with the Israeli Defence Forces. When adopted the vehicle is to be designated the M109A5 and the US Army plans initially to convert almost half of its fleet of 3,500 M109s to this standard while Israel will upgrade all its M109s.

81. Another artillery weapon in widespread NATO service is the M110 8in (203mm) Self-propelled Howitzer; shown here in British colours. With a maximum range of 29,100 metres, the M110 series is capable of firing nuclear projectiles. NATO users include Belgium; Greece; Italy; Netherlands; Spain; Turkey; West Germany as well as the UK and USA.

82. In a rare example of mutual co-operation within NATO, the Multiple Launch Rocket System or MLRS is to be manufactured on two production lines: one in the USA and the other in Europe. Firing a variety of munitions to ranges of about 45 kilometres, MLRS comprises 'six-packs' of rockets on a Self-propelled Launcher Loader (SPLL) which is a variant of the FMC Bradley Fighting Vehicle System. Within NATO MLRS has been adopted by France; Italy; Netherlands; Turkey; West Germany; the UK and USA. Here, an M270 MLRS takes part in Exercise 'Iron Hammer' on trials with the Royal Artillery in the autumn of 1988.

82

83. As part of France's independent nuclear deterrent or 'Force de Frappe', the French Army deploys the Pluton tactical nuclear missile system. Based on the chassis of the AMX-30 MBT, the Pluton launcher vehicle features an integral hydraulic crane for loading and assembling the missile; here, the warhead is about to be fitted.

84. With a tactical nuclear warhead of either 15 or 25 kiloton yield, the Pluton missile has a maximum range of 120 kilometres. It is used only by the French Army which has five regiments (3ème, 4ème, 15ème, 32ème and 74ème Artillerie) of Pluton, each of three batteries with two launchers each.

85. With a similar range to Pluton, Lance is NATO's only other ground-launched tactical nuclear missile system. The equipment comprises two vehicles based on the M548 Tracked Load Carrier, itself a derivative of the M113 APC; the M752 Self-propelled Launcher (SPL) carries the crew of six men and acts as the missile-launcher while the other vehicle is the M688 Loader-Transporter which carries two additional Lance missiles and a crane to reload the SPL.

86

86. In the British Army, the Lance missile system is served by 50 Missile Regiment, Royal Artillery, under the direct control of HQ 1 (Br) Corps and remains in reserve until its nuclear capability is required. Other NATO users of Lance employ warheads with both conventional sub-munitions and nuclear weapons of various yields.

87. Similar in configuration to German wartime reconnaissance vehicles, the *Spähpanzer Luchs* (Lynx) entered service with the Bundeswehr in September 1975. In the Bundeswehr, reconnaissance units are trained to obtain Intelligence of enemy movements by observation rather than by fighting.

88. The M113 APC family has been produced in greater numbers than any other AFV in the Western World with approximately 70,000 having been produced to date. Consequently it remains in widespread service within NATO. Here, an M106A1 4.2in (107mm) Mortar Carrier of the 11th Armored Cavalry Regiment moves through a German town during autumn manoeuvres.

89. One of the most compact fighting vehicles in NATO service is the *Waffenträger* LL-TOW/MK or Wiesel, which has been developed as an airportable family of AFVs for the West German airborne units. This model is the Wiesel MK 20 A1 armed with a Rheinmetall 20mm MK20 Rh 202 cannon in a KUKA gun mount E6-11-A1.

90. In the anti-tank role, Wiesel is fitted with the Hughes TCW 2 (Tube-launched Optically-tracked Wire-guided) ATGW system. With a crew of three, driver, gunner and loader, the Wiesel TOW A1 carries seven missiles of which two are readily to hand. Weighing 2,750 kilograms combat loaded, the Wiesel can be carried slung beneath a helicopter such as the Anglo-French Puma while two can be carried inside a CH-53 or three in a C-130 Hercules.

90

91. Although it has been in service with the British Army for almost forty years, the Ferret armoured car continues to give yeoman service as shown here with 4th Royal Tank Regiment while serving with the United Nations peace-keeping force in Cyprus. The official designation of this model is the Scout Car Reconnaissance Mk 2/3 (Daimler Ferret 4×4) FV701(H).

92. Following widespread and successful use of the Ferret armoured car in North Africa and during the Algerian War of Independence, the French Army issued a requirement for a similar vehicle but with a heavier armament than a single light machine-gun. A design by Panhard was accepted for service as the AML (*Automitrailleuse Légère*) and the first production vehicle was delivered in 1961 – the version illustrated being the AML with HE 60-7 turret.

93. While similar to the previous model, this AML mounts an HE 60-12 turret incorporating a 60mm HB 60 Thomson-Brandt mortar and a 12.7mm (0.5in) heavy machine-gun whereas the HE 60-7 turret mounts the 60mm mortar and twin 7.62mm machine-guns. Weighing 4,800 kilograms, the vehicle carries 43 mortar bombs and 130 rounds of 12.7mm ammunition.

94. Named after a battle in Indo-China, *Dinh Khe* is an AML fitted with an Hispano Suiza H90 turret armed with a 90mm D921 F1 gun which fires HEAT, HE, smoke and canister rounds, as well as a 7.62mm coaxial machine-gun. The Panhard AML has been produced in great numbers and is in service with the armies of at least 37 countries; other NATO users being Portugal and Spain.

95. As a heavy armoured car, the French Army employs the AMX-10RC which equips the reconnaissance regiments at corps level as well as the cavalry regiments of the infantry divisions; each regiment having 36 vehicles. Incorporating many of the automotive components of the tracked AMX-10P IFV, the AMX-10RC is fully amphibious and is armed with a 105mm gun firing HEAT, HE and APFSDS rounds, the latter capable of penetrating many current MBTs. (C. R. Zwart)

96

96. Originally conceived by Panhard as a private venture for the export market, the *Engin de Reconnaissance Canon* (ERC) was adopted by the French Army to equip its Rapid Deployment Force divisions. Designated the ERC 90 F4 Sagaie, each division has 36 vehicles which have replaced the AML 60 and AML 90 4×4 armoured cars.

97. The ERC 90 F4 Sagaie is fitted with a GIAT TS 90 turret mounting a 90mm gun which fires APFSDS, HEAT, HE and canister ammunition, twenty rounds being carried, as well as a coaxial 7.62mm machine-gun. The vehicle is fully amphibious and has six-wheel drive although the centre pair can be raised off the ground when running on prepared roads. The Sagaie also serves with the French Marine Corps and Foreign Legion.

98. With a three-man crew, the *Spähpanzer Luchs* has an all-welded steel hull giving protection against small-arms fire and shell splinters while the turret and hull front are proof against 20mm projectiles. The Luchs itself is armed with a 20mm Rheinmetall Mk20 Rh 202 cannon to the left of which is thermal night vision equipment. The vehicle has no coaxial weapon but a 7.62mm MG3 machine-gun is mounted at the commander's hatch for air and ground defence.

99. Manufactured by Thyssen Henschel, more than 400 *Spähpanzer Luchs* Armoured Amphibious Reconnaissance Vehicles had been procured by the Bundeswehr when production ceased in 1978. As its designation implies, the vehicle is amphibious despite its weight of 19,500 kilograms; being propelled in water by two Schottel steerable propellers at the rear of the hull to a maximum speed of 9km/h.

100

100. Although no longer in front-line service in NATO, the redoubtable AMX-13 represents the alternative tracked configuration for reconnaissance vehicles with its greater cross-country performance. This AMX-13 of the Dutch Army is fitted with an FL-12 turret armed with the same 105mm gun as the AMX-30 MBT.

101. The FV101 Scorpion CVR(T) (Combat Vehicle Reconnaissance Tracked) has been in service with the British Army since 1973 – (cf. *Tanks Illustrated No. 22 Scorpion – The CVR(T) Range*). As the lead vehicle in the CVR(T) family, Scorpion is armed with a 76mm main armament for the fire-support role within reconnaissance regiments. (Tim Neate)

102. Acting as the 'enemy' during an exercise, a Scorpion is typically festooned with extra kit to withstand the rigours of living in the field and with strips of hessian to break up the outline of the vehicle. Above the 76mm gun is a laser designator for engaging and 'destroying' other AFVs during training exercises.

103. As part of the ACE (Allied Command Europe) Mobile Force, the Scorpion, seen here with its sister vehicle the Scimitar, is regularly deployed to Norway to guard the northern flank. The CVR(T) family can operate within a temperature range of −30°C to +50°C without any modification beyond such simple expedients as the perspex windscreen to protect the commander from windchill and the carriage of snowshoes on the side of the vehicle for the crew members.

103

104

105

106

104. Proven in combat during the Falklands War when two Scorpions, four Scimitars and a Samson ARV of the Blues and Royals provided much needed mobility and fire support to the land forces, the Scimitar is the lightest and therefore fastest member of the CVR(T) family. It is seen here with the 13th/18th Hussars during Exercise 'Highwayman' on Salisbury Plain, mounting a GPMG forward of the gunner's position which is an unusual modification.

105. The FV107 Scimitar is armed with a 30mm RARDEN cannon firing a variety of Hispano Suiza Oerlikon ammunition or British rounds in rapid, aimed single shots although bursts of up to six rounds can be fired if necessary against targets such as low-flying aircraft or helicopters. Beside the main armament is a Rank Precision Industries passive night sight with dual magnification for general surveillance and target acquisition.

106. Beside the British Army, other NATO users of the Scorpion family are the Belgian Army (as illustrated); the Spanish Marines and the Royal Air Force which employs Scorpions, Scimitars and Spartans both for airfield defence and for the EOD role by using the 30mm RARDEN to disrupt unexploded bombs and munitions on a runway following an enemy air attack.

107. Of NATO's sixteen nations, only France, Iceland and Luxembourg do not employ variants of the prolific M113 family. The model illustrated is the standard M113A1 diesel-powered APC version seen in service with a unit of Spanish artillery.

108

108. The Bundeswehr is one of the largest users of the M113 after the US Army, and West German industry has developed a number of variants of the basic APC to meet specific battlefield requirements including artillery observation vehicle; armoured air control vehicle; armoured fire control vehicle and armoured artillery control vehicle.

109. With its slab sides and box-like shape, the basic M113 APC is somewhat dated in configuration against which must be set its virtues of reasonable price; ease of operation; reliability and adaptability to innumerable roles. This model is the M113A2 APC which incorporates numerous improvements in what is one of the outstanding AFV designs since the Second World War.

110. A contemporaneous design of the M113, the FV432 APC is similar in configuration but differs in construction in that it is manufactured in steel rather than the aluminium alloy of the M113. Approximately 3,000 vehicles of the FV432 series were built for the British Army; this model mounts the Fox/Scimitar turret armed with the 30mm RARDEN cannon to counter other APCs or IFVs and is shown in the distinctive, disruptive, summer-time camouflage for urban warfare as devised for the AFVs of the Berlin Brigade.

111. The Armoured Personnel Carrier (APC) variant of the CVR(T) family is the FV103 Spartan which can carry four infantrymen in addition to the three-man crew; the infantrymen usually being specialist personnel such as Royal Artillery Blowpipe or Javelin anti-aircraft missile teams or Royal Engineer demolition experts. Standard armament is a single 7.62mm machine-gun mounted on the commander's cupola. (Tim Neate)

112

113

112. Manufactured by OTO Melara of La Spezia, Italy, the Infantry Armoured Fighting Vehicle or IAFV is based on the M113A1 APC but with significant improvements in terms of armour protection and the ability of the transported infantrymen to fire their personal weapons from inside the hull in line with recent tactical doctrine.

113. Designated the VCC-1 or *Camillino* in Italian Army service, the IAFV has a crew of two, commander and driver, and seven infantrymen including one who mans the 12.7mm (0.5in) heavy machine-gun (note the armour plates for the machine-gun have been lowered in this view) while a 7.62mm machine-gun can be mounted on the skid rail at the rear. Protection of the occupants is enhanced by mounting the fuel tanks in external pods each side of the rear ramp.

114. For its particular role of assaulting defended beaches, the US Marine Corps employs purpose-designed APCs designated the Amphibious Assault Vehicle 7 or AAV7 (originally the Landing Vehicle Tracked Personnel Model 7 or LVTP7). Capable of carrying 25 Marines in addition to its crew of three, the AAV7 has a maximum speed in water of 13.5km/h and many improvements such as appliqué armour kits and new weapons stations have been incorporated throughout the fleet.

115. Designed by the Swiss company MOWAG as the Piranha, this vehicle was chosen by the Canadian Armed Forces as the Armoured Vehicle General Purpose (AVGP) for use by both regular and militia units, and 491 units were manufactured by Diesel Division, General Motors of Canada.

116. The AVGP is built in three versions: the Grizzly Wheeled Armoured Personnel Carrier (WAPC) as illustrated; a Fire Support Vehicle mounting an Alvis Scorpion CVR(T) turret named Cougar and a Wheeled Maintenance and Recovery Vehicle (WMRV) named Husky. The Grizzly has a crew of three and carries six infantrymen and is fitted with a Cadillac Gage turret armed with 12.7mm and 7.62mm machine-guns. Subsequently an 8×8 version of this vehicle was chosen by the US Marine Corps for its Light Armored Vehicle (LAV) programme.

117. In the late 1950s, a chassis was designed which was to form the basis for a variety of AFVs including a reconnaissance tank; tank destroyers and an Infantry Combat Vehicle or ICV. Priority was given to the production of the tank destroyers and development of the ICV was not completed until 1969 when it was named Marder. It entered service with the Bundeswehr in 1971. This Marder shows the original configuration with a remote-controlled 7.62mm machine-gun turret mounted on the rear hull top; it is also fitted with a snorkel to allow it to ford to a depth of 2.5 metres.

118. The Marder is armed with the same Rheinmetall 20mm cannon as the *Spähpanzer Luchs* and is fitted with a thermal imaging night sight mounted coaxially. Manufactured by Rheinstahl and Krupp Mak until 1975, 975 Marders were procured by the Bundeswehr. (Pierre Touzin)

119. A disarmed Marder acts as a 'battlefield taxi' to umpires during a field training exercise. The engine compartment is to the right of the driver and houses an MTU MB 833 600hp diesel coupled to a Renk 4-speed planetary gearbox with integral steering and braking systems giving a top speed of 75km/h to a maximum range of 520 kilometres. (Michel Klaver)

118

119

120

121

120. The Marder has a crew of three and carries six infantrymen in the rear hull, four of whom have firing ports to use their weapons from under armour. With the rear-mounted machine-gun now removed, all Marders are currently fitted with a MILAN ATGW launcher, as illustrated, to augment their anti-armour capability. (Pierre Touzin)

121. Developed by the *Atelier de Construction d'Issy-les-Moulineaux* from which the initials AMX derive, the AMX-10P is the current ICV of the French Army and it forms the basis for a variety of other AFVs The AMX-10P also serves with the Greek Army within NATO.

122

122. Production of the AMX-10P began at the *Atelier de Construction Roanne* in 1972 and it entered service with the French Army in 1973. The vehicle mounts a two-man Toucan II turret armed with a 20mm M693 cannon and a co-axial 7.62mm machine-gun. (Pierre Touzin)

123. The AMX-10P has a crew of three comprising driver, gunner and commander, shown at his position on the right-hand side of the Toucan turret. The vehicle is powered by an Hispano-Suiza HS-115 300hp supercharged diesel giving a top speed of 65km/h to a maximum range of 600 kilometres. The AMX-10P is fully amhibious, being propelled in water by two hydrojets at the rear of the hull to a maximum speed of 7km/h. (Pierre Touzin)

123

124

125

124. In addition to the three-man crew, the AMX-10P carries eight infantrymen who enter and leave the vehicle by the electrically operated ramp at the rear which incorporates two doors, each with a firing port. Among the stores shown that are carried inside the vehicle are the 760 20mm rounds for the main armament and 2,000 7.62mm rounds for the co-axial machine-gun.

125. A radically improved version of the M113A1 APC incorporating increased armour protection, an enclosed weapons station and firing ports for the infantrymen in the rear hull, the Armoured Infantry Fighting Vehicle or AIFV is used by Belgium and the Netherlands within NATO and is currently being produced in Turkey for the Turkish Army.

126. The M2 Infantry Fighting Vehicle and its sister vehicle the M3 Cavalry Fighting Vehicle have been designed to accompany the current US Army MBT, the M1 Abrams, on the modern battlefield. Named in honour of the late General of the Army, Omar Bradley, the M2 IFV entered service in 1982.

127. At 22,590 kilograms combat loaded, the M2 Bradley is a large and powerful machine incorporating considerable protection in the form of spaced laminate and the latest aluminium alloy armour together with formidable firepower, notwithstanding a power-to-weight ratio of 20.4hp/tonne which gives high mobility. (Pierre Touzin)

128. The M2 Bradley carries seven infantrymen in the rear hull as well as a crew of three comprising driver, gunner and commander who dismounts with the infantry for ground action. For mounted action, six firing ports are provided, two each side and two to the rear from which the infantrymen fire their M231 5.56mm automatic weapons. The M2 is fully amphibious, being propelled in water by its tracks.

129. The US Army has a requirement for 6,889 M2 and M3 vehicles but the Bradley will not replace the M113 APC on a one-for-one basis since the latter will remain in its supporting roles for many years to come. Here, an early model M2 of 3rd Infantry Division moves through wooded terrain during an exercise in Germany.

130. An M3 Cavalry Fighting Vehicle of 11th Armored

Cavalry Regiment displays its excellent cross-country mobility thanks to its Cummins VTA-903T turbocharged 500hp diesel coupled to a General Electric HMPT-5000 hydro-mechanical transmission with a top speed of 66km/h to a range of 483 kilometres. The M3 Bradley is virtually identical with the M2 except that it has a crew of five and is configured for the reconnaissance role as a scout vehicle with blanked off firing ports and greatly increased ammunition stowage.

130

131. During production many improvements have been incorporated; one of the most important being the fitting of the Hughes TOW 2 ATGW in the two-man TBAT-11 or TOW/Bushmaster Armored Turret which gives the Bradley its powerful firepower as shown on this M2A1 with its TOW launcher raised for firing against armoured targets out to a range of 3,750 metres. The main armament is the Bushmaster M242 25mm Chain Gun with a 7.62mm M240C machine-gun mounted coaxially. The M2 carries 900 25mm rounds and 2,340 rounds of 7.62mm ammunition.

131

132. The latest model of the Bradley is the M2A2 which has improved armour for both the hull and turret with the addition of reactive-explosive blocks; revised internal stowage of fuel and ammunition; spall liners to protect the crew further and an improved smoke-screening system. This increases weight considerably necessitating a greater engine output of 600hp; a loss of its amphibious capability and the deletion of the hull firing ports. This M2A2 lacks the reactive armour blocks which would only be fitted during wartime.

132

133. As a replacement for the FV432 APC, design work began in 1977 of the MCV-80 (Mechanized Combat Vehicle of the 80s) and development was undertaken by GKN Sankey who were awarded a production contract in 1984. The first production vehicle, now named Warrior, was handed over to the British Army in May 1987 and the first mechanized battalion in BAOR was fully operational with Warrior in mid 1988.

134. At 24,500 kilograms combat loaded, Warrior is the heaviest of the current generation of IFVs reflecting the importance the British Army attaches to armour protection coupled with a powerful main armament in the 30mm RARDEN cannon and coaxial 7.62mm L94A1 Chain Gun. Here, a Warrior is decontaminated during an NBC exercise. (Tim Neate)

135. In British Army service the standard IFV is known as a 'section vehicle' since it carries eight infantrymen (one of whom commands the vehicle and dismounts with the infantry) as well as the driver and gunner. Warrior also carries all the weapons and stores, including a chemical lavatory, required to fight on the battlefield for up to 48 hours.

136. The first prototype of the VCC-80 IFV undergoes troop trials with the Italian Army. Developed by OTO Melara and IVECO FIAT, the VCC-80 is a compact vehicle, being only 2.25 metres to the top of the turret, with a crew of three. The troop compartment holds six infantrymen and incorporates five firing ports, two each side and one in the rear ramp. The FIAT turbocharged diesel develops 480bhp giving the VCC-80 an excellent power-to-weight ratio of 25bhp/tonne and a maximum speed of 70km/h to a range of 600 kilometres.

137. In the face of the perceived threat of overwhelming Warsaw Pact superiority in numbers of AFVs, the NATO armies have responded with the widespread deployment of ATGW systems which, to increase mobility and protection, are increasingly mounted on AFVs such as this Hughes TOW on an AMX *Véhicule de Combat d'Infanterie* of the Dutch Army; the same vehicle mounting a MILAN ATGW launcher is used by the Belgian Army.

138. In the Italian Army, the M113A1 APC, built under licence by OTO Melara of La Spezia, has been fitted with a pedestal-mounted TOW ATGW system which when not required can be retracted into the troop compartment where additional missiles are also stored. This vehicle is designated the XM233E1 TOW Missile Carrier.

139. A recent variant of the CVR(T) family is the Spartan APC fitted with the Euromissile MILAN ATGW system. It comprises two ready-to-fire missiles on a MILAN Compact Turret (MCT) installed over the roof. A standard MILAN firing post is

139

140

also carried so that it can be deployed away from the vehicle if required. (Tim Neate)

140. With a further eleven missiles carried internally, the Spartan MCT entered service with the British Army in September 1986, and each mechanized infantry battalion in BAOR has four such vehicles to improve its anti-armour capability. (Tim Neate)

141. Similar in appearance from the front to the Spartan is the FV102 Striker ATGW (Anti-Tank Guided Weapon) vehicle which serves with the anti-armour units of the Royal Armoured Corps. Beside the commander's No. 26 cupola is the gunner's split-view monocular sight with magnifications of ×1 for observation and ×10 for engaging targets out to a range of 4,000 metres. It also incorporates a Barr and Stroud thermal imaging night sight. (Tim Neate)

142. The most obvious difference between the Spartan and the Striker is the latter's launcher assembly at the rear for five British Aerospace Swingfire ATGW missiles. A further five missiles are carried inside the hull which are loaded manually into the launcher boxes by a crew member outside the vehicle. A troop of four Strikers serves in armoured regiments and four troops within an armoured reconnaissance regiment. (Tim Neate)

141

142

143. The M901A1 Improved TOW Vehicle (ITV) is an M113A2 fitted with the TOW Under Armor System designed by Emerson Electric Company. The M901 entered service with the US Army in 1979 and 2,992 ITVs have been procured. The system has far greater survivability than the simple mounting of an ATGW launcher on the roof of an APC.

144. The armoured launcher assembly, known as the Hammerhead, incorporates two TOW launch tubes; the TOW sight assembly and the acquisition sight mounted on two elevating arms with limits of +34° and −30° and 360° traverse so that it can operate on uphill or downhill slopes or on lateral embankments. An additional ten missiles are carried in the hull and the launcher tubes can be reloaded from under armour protection in 40 seconds.

145. When not in use the launcher assembly is traversed through 180° and lowered so that from a distance it appears much like a standard APC. However it can be brought into operation within 20 seconds. The crew comprises driver, gunner, commander and one or two missile handlers depending on the mission. The extra weight of the weapon system does not impair the vehicle's amphibious capability or cross-country mobility. (Pierre Touzin)

146. The TOW Under Armor system has been applied to a variety of other vehicles such as the Italian VCC-1 which was sold to Saudi Arabia and, as illustrated, on the FMC Armoured Infantry Fighting Vehicle. This version has been procured by the Dutch Army as the YPR 765 PRAT (*Pantser Rups* Anti-Tank) which entered service in 1982. The TOW equipment can be dismounted from the vehicle and set up on a ground mounting, ready to fire, in under one minute.

147. Virtually identical in appearance with the ITV, an M981 Fire Support Team Vehicle (FISTV) takes up a typical hulldown position with only the 'Hammerhead' exposed as it undertakes its mission of locating and designating targets and then communicating accurate target information to artillery and helicopter support units, particularly those with laser-guided munitions such as Copperhead and Hellfire.

145

146

147

148. Using the same elevating mechanism as the ITV, the M981 FISTV incorporates the AN/TVQ-2 GLLD (Ground Laser Locator/ Designator); AN/TAS-4 Night Sight; north-seeking gyrocompass; land navigation system and extensive communications equipment embodied in an M113A2 with externally mounted fuel cells at the rear which, together with the number of radio antennae, are the most noticeable differences from the ITV. The US Army has a requirement for 970 FISTVs.

149. Following in the tradition of wartime tank destroyers, the newly formed Bundeswehr issued a requirement for a 90mm self-propelled anti-tank gun which, after prolonged trials, emerged as the *Jagdpanzer Kanone* or JPZ 4–5 in 1965. A total of 750 vehicles were built from 1965 to 1967, production being shared between Hanomag and Henschel. (Pierre Touzin)

150. With a firing simulator mounted above its 90mm gun, a *Jagdpanzer Kanone* advances through a smoke-screen during a field training exercise. Weighing 2,750 kilograms the JPZ 4–5 is powered by a Daimler Benz MB 837 500hp diesel and Renk HSWL 123 transmission giving a top speed of 70km/h to a range of 400 kilometres. Eighty improved versions of the *Jagdpanzer Kanone* were produced by Belgium from 1975 and eight Belgian infantry battalions have two platoons of four vehicles each with the remaining sixteen being used for training.

151. The 90mm main armament fires the same types of ammunition as the M47 and M48, which were the first tanks issued to the Bundeswehr, to an effective range of 2,000 metres at a maximum rate of fire of twelve rounds a minute. Recently a number of *Jagdpanzer Kanone* have had their 90mm gun removed so that the vehicles can be used in the artillery observation post role while another 162 have been converted to become *Jagdpanzer Rakete* or Jaguar 2 armed with Hughes TOW ATGW systems.

152. In 1967 the *Jagdpanzer Rakete* succeeded the *Jagdpanzer Kanone* on the production lines at Hanomag and Henschel and 370 had been built by the following year. Originally these were fitted with the Aérospatiale SS-11 wire-guided ATGW system with a maximum range of 3,000 metres, but from 1978 316 vehicles were rebuilt with the Euromissile K35 HOT ATGW system with a maximum range of 4,000 metres.

153. The *Jagdpanzer Rakete* armed with HOT is now named Jaguar 1 and incorporates distinctive, spaced armour plates bolted to the front and sides of the hull. Secondary armament comprises a bow-mounted 7.62mm machine-gun and one at the commander's cupola as well as a bank of eight smoke dischargers across the rear decks.

154. When fitted with the Hughes TOW ATGW system the *Jagdpanzer Rakete* is known as the Jaguar 2. Converted from *Jagdpanzer Kanone*, the Jaguar 2 mounts the TOW system with its integral AN/TAS-4 night sight because it is significantly cheaper than HOT. The conversions were undertaken between 1983 and 1985. (Pierre Touzin)

155

155. In the air defence role, the French Army uses a variant of the AMX-13 designated the AMX-13 DCA (*Défense Contre Avions*). The vehicle incorporates a SAMM S 401A turret housing two Hispano-Suiza HSS-831A 30mm automatic cannon and the Thomsom-CSF coherent pulse-Doppler DR-VC-1A Oeil Noir 1 (Black Eye) radar. 60 AMX-13 DCA vehicles were procured by the French Army.

156. The two HSS-831A 30mm guns have a maximum elevation of +85°, a depression of −5° and the turret can be rotated through 360°. Once a target has been acquired, the gunner can select single shots, five or 15-round bursts or fully automatic from either gun or both together at a cyclic rate of 600rpm per barrel. Each belt-fed gun has 300 rounds of 30mm ammunition and an effective range of 3,500 metres.

157. In service with the US Army since 1968, the M163 20mm Vulcan Self-Propelled Anti-Aircraft Gun System saw limited action during the Vietnam War in the ground support role. The M163 is currently deployed in US service in composite air-defence battalions with the Chaparal SAM system; a battalion having 24 of each. (Pierre Touzin)

158. The six-barrelled 20mm M61A1 rotary cannon is of the 'Gatling gun' type and has two rates of fire: 1,000 rounds per minute against ground targets and 3,000 against aircraft. Maximum effective anti-aircraft range is 1,600 metres. The system has recently been upgraded with an improved fire control system and new ammunition which is effective to 2,600 metres; this version is designated M163A2. Approximately 389 M163 vehicles remain in service with the US Army. (Pierre Touzin)

159. For area defence against aircraft the British Army employs the Towed Rapier, but for the protection of armoured units in the forward battle area the system is mounted on the M548 cargo-carrier variant of the M113 APC family to become Tracked Rapier which carries eight ready-to-fire missiles in armoured bins, that can be fired within 30 seconds of coming to a halt. It is operated by a crew of three who are housed in an armoured cab at the front.

160. The latest air-defence system about to enter service with the British Army is the Starstreak Low-Altitude Self-Propelled High Velocity Missile System developed by Shorts of Belfast. Mounted on an enlarged version of the Spartan APC known as Stormer, the Starstreak missile comprises three fin-stabilized high-density darts which separate into triangular formation in flight to give a much increased hit probability against low-flying and sudden appearing ground-attack aircraft.

160

161. In a collaborative effort between Aérospatiale of France and Messerschmidt-Bölkow-Blohm of West Germany, now jointly known as Euromissile, development of a low-altitude SAM system began in 1964. Known as Roland, the system comes in two versions: Roland 1 for clear-weather conditions and Roland 2 as the all-weather variant (latterly an improved model called Roland 3).

162. The West German version of Roland is mounted on a modified Marder chassis. A total of 140 systems were procured by the Bundeswehr and they serve with three air defence regiments (100th, 200th and 300th) with 36 firing units in each. The missile is controlled either optically or by radar and has been designed to engage aircraft at altitudes between 20 and 3,000 metres and at ranges between 500 and a maximum of 6,300 metres; although an Argentinian firing unit at Port Stanley shot down a Sea Harrier during the Falklands War at an altitude of 3,962 metres and a range of 11,200 metres.

163. In the French Army, Roland is mounted on a modified AMX-30 chassis designated AMX-30R and 200 are in service. Employed at corps level, the 53rd, 57th and 58th Roland regiments are organized into four batteries each with eight firing units while the 51st Air Defence Regiment is a composite formation with three Roland batteries and a battery of AMX-13DCA guns. The USAF also uses Roland to defend three of its bases in West Germany.

164

164. Development of a self-propelled, all-weather, anti-aircraft gun for the Bundeswehr began in 1965. Based on a lengthened chassis of the Leopard 1 MBT, the design incorporated twin 35mm Oerlikon cannon and emerged as the *Gepard* (Cheetah). In September 1973, an order was placed for 420 *Gepards* and the first production vehicles entered service in 1976. The Belgian Army also employs the *Gepard* and 55 are currently in service.

165

165. The *Gepard* features a Siemens MPDR-12 fully coherent pulse-Doppler search radar at the rear which can function while the vehicle is in motion to detect aircraft out of range of 15 kilometres. Once a target has been detected and identified, the information is passed to the coherent Siemens-Albis pulse-Doppler tracking radar mounted on the front of the turret which, with the aid of an analogue computer, automatically lays the guns on the target. (Pierre Touzin)

166

166. The two Oerlikon 35mm KDA cannon have a cyclic rate of 550 rounds per minute per barrel and normally open fire when an enemy aircraft is between 3,000 and 4,000 metres away with a normal burst consisting of 20 to 40 rounds. The guns are belt-fed and the empty cartridge cases are automatically ejected outside the turret.

167. In 1969 the Dutch Army ordered a version of the *Gepard* but fitted with a Hollandse Signaalapparaten integrated Ka-band monopulse-Doppler surveillance and tracking radar. A total of 95 vehicles were procured between 1977 and 1979. Originally known as the CA-1, it is now designated the *Pantser Rups Tegen Luchdoelen* (PRTL) but is more commonly called Cheetah.

168. Both *Gepard* and Cheetah carry a total of 660 rounds of ammunition with 310 anti-aircraft high-explosive incendiary rounds and twenty rounds of armour-piercing ammunition per cannon; the latter carried externally in armoured bins outboard of the gun mountings. The gunner can select either AA or AP ammunition at the flick of a switch and fire single shots, bursts or continuous fire.

169. Developed by the Swiss company Oerlikon-Bührle, the ADATS missile system was designed to counter both air and ground targets but its primary role is air defence whereas its anti-tank capability is very much a last resort measure, although the warhead can penetrate 100 centimetres of steel armour. ADATS has been adopted by the Canadian Armed Forces and more recently by the US Army which has a requirement for 562 firing units. Mounted on an M3A1 Bradley chassis, the ADATS also has a McDonnell Douglas Helicopters 25mm Chain Gun mounted on top as shown here.

170. Developed by OTO Melara, the Italian Army is currently procuring a quadruple 25mm self-propelled anti-aircraft system with 340 on order. The system comprises a one-man aluminium alloy turret with four externally mounted Oerlikon-Italiana 25mm KBA-B cannon mounted on a modified M113 APC.

171. Known as the SIDAM 25, the vehicle has a crew of three and the four 25mm guns have a rate of fire of 2,400 rounds per minute which, with the 600 ready rounds carried, allows eight two-second bursts to a maximum range of 2,500 metres. A further 30 APDS ready rounds are carried for anti-armour ground defence.

171